DON

St Laurence Poultney

St Anthonies

the Ex

the Exch ange

Olde Swann

Fishmongers h

FLUVIUS

South   Winchester house   Warke

St. Dunston in the east

St. Hellen:

St. Andrew

THE BRIDGE

St. Mary Oueris

Mr William Shakspeares Comedies, Histories & Tragedies – the book we now know as the First Folio – hit the London booksellers in autumn 1623. It's hard to overstate its impact and significance. Seven years after Shakespeare's death, it gathered thirty-six plays, half of them printed here for the first time. These might well have been lost were it not for the First Folio: no 'Friends, Romans and countrymen', no 'double, double, toil and trouble', no 'if music be the food of love, play on'. Without the First Folio's title-page portrait, we would have no image of Shakespeare authenticated by those who knew him, including his friends and fellow actors John Heminge and Henry Condell, and Ben Jonson, the dramatist who recognised that his talented rival was 'not of an age, but for all time'. And without this weighty book, Shakespeare's reputation could not have translated from stage to page, from entertainment to literature, and from London's theatre district to the world. What's special about the Bodleian Library copy is the signs of use: this is not a perfect museum piece but a working document, marked – literally – by some of the readers whose own creativity has been inspired by its contents.

Oxford, Bodleian Library, Arch. G c.7

A CATALOGVE

of the feuerall Comedies, Hiftories, and Tragedies contained in this Volume.

The Comedie of Errors.

Actus primus, Scena prima.

Enter the Duke of Ephesus , with the Merchant of Siracusa,
Iaylor, and other attendants.

Marchant.

PRoceed *Solinus* to procure my fall,
And by the doome of death end woes and all.

Duke. Merchant of *Siracusa*, plead no more.
I am not partiall to infringe our Lawes;
The enmity and discord which of late
Sprung from the rancorous outrage of your Duke,
To Merchants our well-dealing Countrimen,
Who wanting gilders to redeeme their liues,
Haue seal'd his rigorous statutes with their blouds,
Excludes all pitty from our threatning lookes:
For since the mortall and intestine iarres
Twixt thy seditious Countrimen and vs,
It hath in solemne Synodes beene decreed,
Both by the *Siracusians* and our selues,
To admit no trafficke to our aduerse townes:
Nay more, if any borne at *Ephesus*
Be seene at any *Siracusian* Marts and Fayres:
Againe, if any *Siracusian* borne
Come to the Bay of *Ephesus*, he dies:
His goods confiscate to the Dukes dispose,
Vnlesse a thousand markes be leuied
To quit the penalty, and to ransome him:
Thy substance, valued at the highest rate,
Cannot amount vnto a hundred Markes,
Therefore by Law thou art condemn'd to die.

Mer. Yet this my comfort, when your words are done,
My woes end likewise with the euening Sonne.

Duk. Well *Siracusian*, say in briefe the cause
Why thou departedst from thy natiue home?
And for what cause thou cam'st to *Ephesus*.

Mer. A heauier taske could not haue beene impos'd,
Then I to speake my griefes vnspeakeable:
Yet that the world may witnesse that my end
Was wrought by nature, not by vile offence,
Ile vtter what my sorrow giues me leaue.
In *Syracusa* was I borne, and wedde
Vnto a woman, happy but for me,
And by me; had not our hap beene bad:
With her I liu'd in ioy, our wealth increast
By prosperous voyages I often made
To *Epidamium*, till my factors death,
And he great care of goods at randone left,
Drew me from kinde embracements of my spouse;
From whom my absence was not fixe moneths olde,
Before her selfe (almost at fainting vnder

The pleasing punishment that women beare)
Had made prouision for her following me,
And soone, and safe, arriued where I was:
There had she not beene long, but she became
A ioyfull mother of two goodly sonnes:
And, which was strange, the one so like the other,
As could not be distinguish'd but by names.
That very howre, and in the selfe-same Inne,
A meane woman was deliuered
Of such a burthen Male, twins both alike:
Those, for their parents were exceeding poore,
I bought, and brought vp to attend my sonnes.
My wife, not meanely prowd of two such boyes,
Made daily motions for our home returne:
Vnwilling I agreed, alas, too soone wee came aboord.
A league from *Epidamium* had we saild
Before the alwaies winde-obeying deepe
Gaue any Tragicke Instance of our harme:
But longer did we not retaine much hope;
For what obscured light the heauens did grant,
Did but conuay vnto our fearefull mindes
A doubtfull warrant of immediate death,
Which though my selfe would gladly haue imbrac'd,
Yet the incessant weepings of my wife,
Weeping before for what she saw must come,
And piteous playnings of the prettie babes
That mourn'd for fashion, ignorant what to feare,
Forst me to seeke delayes for them and me,
And this it was: (for other meanes was none)
The Sailors sought for safety by our boate,
And left the ship then sinking ripe to vs:
My wife, more carefull for the latter borne,
Had fastned him vnto a small spare Mast,
Such as sea-faring men prouide for stormes:
To him one of the other twins was bound,
Whil'st I had beene like heedfull of the other.
The children thus dispos'd, my wife and I,
Fixing our eyes on whom our care was fixt,
Fastned our selues at eyther end the mast,
And floating straight, obedient to the streame,
Was carried towards *Corinth*, as we thought.
At length the sonne gazing vpon the earth,
Disperst those vapours that offended vs,
And by the benefit of his wished light
The seas waxt calme, and we discouered
Two shippes from farre, making amaine to vs:
Of *Corinth* that, of *Epidarus* this,
But ere they came, oh let me say no more,
Gather the sequell by that went before.

Duk. Nay forward old man, doe not breake off so,

The first Part of Henry the Sixt.

Actus Primus. Scœna Prima.

Dead March.

Enter the Funerall of King Henry the Fift, attended on by the Duke of Bedford, Regent of France ; the Duke of Gloster, Protector; the Duke of Exeter Warwicke, the Bishop of Winchester, and the Duke of Somerset.

Bedford.

Vng be ỹ heauens with black,yield day to night;
Comets importing change of Times and States,
Brandish your cryſtall Treſſes in the Skie,
And with them ſcourge the bad reuolting Stars,
That haue conſented vnto *Henries* death:
King *Henry* the Fift,too famous to liue long,
England ne're loſt a King of ſo much worth.

Gloſt. England ne're had a King vntill his time:
Vertue he had,deſeruing to command,
His brandiſht Sword did blinde men with his beames,
His Armes ſpred wider then a Dragons Wings :
His ſparkling Eyes,repleat with wrathfull fire,
More dazled and droue back his Enemies,
Then mid-day Sunne,fierce bent againſt their faces.
What ſhould I ſay? his Deeds exceed all ſpeech :
He ne're lif: vp his Hand,but conquered.

*Exe.*We mourne in black,why mourn we not in blood?
Henry is dead,and neuer ſhall reuiue :
Vpon a Wodden Coffin we attend;
And Deaths diſhonourable Victorie,
We with our ſtately preſence glorifie,
Like Captiues bound to a Triumphant Carre.
What? ſhall we curſe the Planets of Miſhap,
That plotted thus our Glories ouerthrow?
Or ſhall we thinke the ſubtile-witted French,
Coniurers and Sorcerers, that afraid of him,
By Magick Verſes haue contriu'd his end.

Winch. He was a King,bleſt of the King of Kings.
Vnto the French,the dreadfull Iudgement-Day
So dreadfull will not be,as was his ſight.
The Battailes of the Lord of Hoſts he fought :
The Churches Prayers made him ſo proſperous.

Gloſt. The Church ? where is it ?
Had not Church-men pray'd,
His thred of Life had not ſo ſoone decay'd.
None doe you like, but an effeminate Prince,
Whom like a Schoole-boy you may ouer-awe.

*Winch. Gloſter,*what ere we like,thou art Protector,
And lookeſt to command the Prince and Realme.
Thy Wife is prowd, ſhe holdeth thee in awe,
More then God or Religious Church-men may.

Gloſt. Name not Religion,for thou lou'ſt the Fleſh,
And ne're throughout the yeere to Church thou go'ſt,
Except it be to pray againſt thy foes.

*Bed.*Ceaſe,ceaſe theſe Iarres,& reſt your minds in peace:
Let's to the Altar : Heralds wayt on vs;
In ſtead of Gold,wee'le offer vp our Armes,
Since Armes auayle not,now that *Henry's* dead,
Poſteritie await for wretched yeeres,
When at their Mothers moiſtned eyes,Babes ſhall ſuck,
Our Ile be made a Nouriſh of ſalt Teares,
And none but Women left to wayle the dead.
Henry the Fift,thy Ghoſt I inuocate :
Proſper this Realme, keepe it from Ciuill Broyles,
Combat with aduerſe Planets in the Heauens;
A farre more glorious Starre thy Soule will make,
Then *Iulius Cæſar,*or bright----

Enter a Meſſenger.

Meſſ. My honourable Lords,health to you all :
Sad tidings bring I to you out of France,
Of loſſe, of ſlaughter,and diſcomfiture :
Guyen,Champaigne,Rheimes,Orleance,
Paris Guytors,Poictiers,are all quite loſt.

Bedf. What ſay'ſt thou man,before dead *Henry's* Coarſe?
Speake ſoftly,or the loſſe of thoſe great Townes
Will make him burſt his Lead,and riſe from death.

Gloſt. Is Paris loſt? is Roan yeelded vp ?
If *Henry* were recall'd to life againe,
Theſe news would cauſe him once more yeeld the Ghoſt.

Exe. How were they loſt ? what trecherie was vs'd?
Meſſ. No trecherie, but want of Men and Money.
Amongſt the Souldiers this is muttered,
That here you maintaine ſeuerall Factions :
And whil'ſt a Field ſhould be diſpatcht and fought,
You are diſputing of your Generals.
One would haue lingring Warres,with little coſt ;
Another would flye ſwift,but wanteth Wings :
A third thinkes,without expence at all,
By guilefull faire words,Peace may be obtayn'd.
Awake,awake,Engliſh Nobilitie,
Let not ſlouth dimme your Honors,new begot ;
Cropt are the Flower-de-Luces in your Armes
Of Englands Coat,one halfe is cut away.

Exe. Were our Teares wanting to this Funerall,
Theſe Tidings would call forth her flowing Tides.

Bedf. Me they concerne,Regent I am of France :
Giue me my ſteeled Coat,Ile fight for France.
Away with theſe diſgracefull wayling Robes ;
Wounds will I lend the French,in ſtead of Eyes,
To weepe their intermiſſiue Miſeries.

Enter

Much adoe about Nothing.

Actus primus, Scena prima.

Enter Leonato Gouernour of Messina, Innogen his wife, Hero his daughter, and Beatrice his Neece, with a messenger.

Leonato.

Learne in this Letter, that *Don Peter* of *Arragon*, comes this night to *Messina*.

Mess. He is very neere by this : he was not three Leagues off when I left him.

Leon. How many Gentlemen haue you lost in this action?

Mess. But few of any sort, and none of name.

Leon. A victorie is twice it selfe, when the atchieuer brings home full numbers : I finde heere, that Don *Peter* hath bestowed much honor on a yong *Florentine*, called *Claudio*.

Mess. Much deseru'd on his part, and equally remembred by Don *Pedro*, he hath borne himselfe beyond the promise of his age, doing in the figure of a Lambe, the feats of a Lion, he hath indeede better bettred expectation, then you must expect of me to tell you how.

Leo. He hath an Vnckle heere in *Messina*, wil be very much glad of it.

Mess. I haue alreadie deliuered him letters, and there appeares much ioy in him, euen so much, that ioy could not shew it selfe modest enough, without a badg of bitternesse.

Leo. Did he breake out into teares ?

Mess. In great measure.

Leo. A kinde ouerflow of kindnesse, there are no faces truer, then those that are so wash'd, how much better is it to weepe at ioy, then to ioy at weeping?

Bea. I pray you, is Signior *Mountanto* return'd from the warres, or no ?

Mess. I know none of that name, Lady, there was none such in the armie of any sort.

Leon. What is he that you aske for Neece?

Hero. My cousin meanes Signior Benedick of *Padua*.

Mess. O he's return'd, and as pleasant as euer he was.

Beat. He set vp his bils here in *Messina*, & challeng'd Cupid at the Flight : and my Vnckles foole reading the Challenge, subscrib'd for Cupid, and challeng'd him at the Burbolt. I pray you, how many hath hee kil'd and eaten in these warres? But how many hath he kil'd? for indeed, I promis'd to eate all of his killing.

Leon. 'Faith Neece, you taxe Signior Benedicke too much, but hee'l be meet with you, I doubt it not.

Mess. He hath done good seruice Lady in these wars.

Beat. You had musty victuall, and he hath holpe to ease it : he's a very valiant Trencher-man, hee hath an excellent stomacke.

Mess. And a good souldier too Lady.

Beat. And a good souldier to a Lady. But what is he to a Lord ?

Mess. A Lord to a Lord, a man to a man, stuft with all honourable vertues.

Beat. It is so indeed, he is no lesse then a stuft man : but for the stuffing well, we are all mortall.

Leon. You must not (sir) mistake my Neece, there is a kind of merry war betwixt Signior Benedick, & her : they neuer meet, but there's a skirmish of wit betweene them.

Bea. Alas, he gets nothing by that. In our last conflict, foure of his fiue wits went halting off, and now is the whole man gouern'd with one : so that if hee haue wit enough to keepe himselfe warme, let him beare it for a difference betweene himselfe and his horse : For it is all the wealth that he hath left, to be knowne a reasonable creature. Who is his companion now? He hath euery month a new sworne brother.

Mess. I'st possible ?

Beat. Very easily possible : he weares his faith but as the fashion of his hat, it euer changes with the next block.

Mess. I see (Lady) the Gentleman is not in your bookes.

Bea. No, and he were, I would burne my study : But I pray you, who is his companion ? Is there no young squarer now, that will make a voyage with him to the diuell ?

Mess. He is most in the company of the right noble *Claudio.*

Beat. O Lord, he will hang vpon him like a disease : he is sooner caught then the pestilence, and the taker runs presently mad. God helpe the noble *Claudio*, if hee haue caught the Benedict, it will cost him a thousand pound ere he be cur'd.

Mess. I will hold friends with you Lady.

Bea. Do good friend.

Leo. You'l ne're run mad Neece.

Bea. No, not till a hot Ianuary.

Mess. Don *Pedro* is approach'd.

Enter don Pedro, Claudio, Benedicke, Balthasar, and Iohn the bastard.

Pedro. Good Signior *Leonato*, you are come to meet your trouble : the fashion of the world is to auoid cost, and you encounter it.

Leon. Neuer came trouble to my house in the likenes of your Grace : for trouble being gone, comfort should remaine : but when you depart from me, sorrow abides, and happinesse takes his leaue.

A MIDSOMMER
Nights Dreame.

Actus primus.

Enter Theseus, Hippolita, with others.

Theseus.

Ow faire Hippolita, our nuptiall houre
Drawes on apace: foure happy daies bring in
Another Moon: but oh, me thinkes, how flow
This old Moon wanes; She lingers my defires
Like to a Step-dame, or a Dowager,
Long withering out a yong mans reuennew.

Hip. Foure daies wil quickly fteep thefelues in nights
Foure nights wil quickly dreame away the time:
And then the Moone, like to a filuer bow,
Now bent in heauen, fhal behold the night
Of our folemnities.

The. Go Philoftrate,
Stirre vp the Athenian youth to merriments,
Awake the pert and nimble fpirit of mirth,
Turne melancholy forth to Funerals:
The pale companion is not for our pompe,
Hippolita, I woo'd thee with my fword,
And wonne thy loue, doing thee iniuries:
But I will wed thee in another key,
With pompe, with triumph, and with reuelling.

Enter Egeus and his daughter Hermia, Lyfander,
and Demetrius.

Ege. Happy be *Theseus*, our renowned Duke.

The. Thanks good *Egeus*: what's the news with thee?

Ege. Full of vexation, come I, with complaint
Againft my childe, my daughter *Hermia*.
Stand forth *Demetrius*.
My Noble Lord,
This man hath my confent to marrie her.
Stand forth *Lyfander*.
And my gracious Duke,
This man hath bewitch'd the bofome of my childe:
Thou, thou *Lyfander*, thou haft giuen her rimes,
And interchang'd loue-tokens with my childe:
Thou haft by Moone-light at her window fung,
With faining voice, verfes of faining loue,
And ftolne the impreffion of her fantafie,
With bracelets of thy haire, rings, gawdes, conceits,
Knackes, trifles, Nofe-gaies, fweet meats (meffengers
Of ftrong preuailment in vnhardned youth)

With cunning haft thou filch'd my daughters heart,
Turn'd her obedience (which is due to me)
To ftubborne harfhneffe. And my gracious Duke,
Be it fo fhe will not heere before your Grace,
Confent to marrie with *Demetrius*,
I beg the ancient priuiledge of Athens;
As fhe is mine, I may difpofe of her;
Which fhall be either to this Gentleman,
Or to her death, according to our Law,
Immediately prouided in that cafe.

The. What fay you *Hermia*? be aduis'd faire Maide,
To you your Father fhould be as a God;
One that compos'd your beauties; yea and one
To whom you are but as a forme in waxe
By him imprinted: and within his power,
To leaue the figure, or disfigure it:
Demetrius is a worthy Gentleman.

Her. So is *Lyfander*.

The. In himfelfe he is.
But in this kinde, wanting your fathers voyce,
The other muft be held the worthier.

Her. I would my father look'd but with my eyes.

The. Rather your eies muft with his iudgment looke.

Her. I do entreat your Grace to pardon me.
I know not by what power I am made bold,
Nor how it may concerne my modeftie
In fuch a prefence heere to pleade my thoughts:
But I befeech your Grace, that I may know
The worft that may befall me in this cafe,
If I refufe to wed *Demetrius*.

The. Either to dye the death, or to abiure
For euer the fociety of men.
Therefore faire *Hermia* queftion your defires,
Know of your youth, examine well your blood,
Whether (if you yeeld not to your fathers choice)
You can endure the liuerie of a Nunne,
For aye to be in fhady Cloifter mew'd,
To liue a barren fifter all your life,
Chanting faint hymnes to the cold fruitleffe Moone,
Thrice bleffed they that mafter fo their blood,
To vndergo fuch maiden pilgrimage,
But earthlier happie is the Rofe diftil'd,
Then that which withering on the virgin thorne,
Growes, liues, and dies, in fingle bleffedneffe.

N   *Her.*

152

THE TRAGEDIE OF
HAMLET, Prince of Denmarke.

Actus Primus. Scœna Prima.

Enter Barnardo and Francisco two Centinels.

Barnardo.

Ho's there?

Fran. Nay answer me: Stand & vnfold your selfe.

Bar. Long liue the King.

Fran. Barnardo?

Bar. He.

Fran. You come most carefully vpon your houre.

Bar. 'Tis now strook twelue, get thee to bed Francisco.

Fran. For this releefe much thankes: 'Tis bitter cold, And I am sicke at heart.

Barn. Haue you had quiet Guard?

Fran. Not a Mouse stirring.

Barn. Well, goodnight. If you do meet Horatio and Marcellus, the Riuals of my Watch, bid them make hast.

Enter Horatio and Marcellus.

Fran. I thinke I heare them. Stand: who's there?

Hor. Friends to this ground.

Mar. And Leige-men to the Dane.

Fran. Giue you good night.

Mar. O farwel honest Soldier, who hath relieu'd you?

Fra. Barnardo ha's my place: giue you goodnight.

Exit Fran.

Mar. Holla Barnardo.

Bar. Say, what is Horatio there?

Hor. A peece of him.

Bar. Welcome Horatio, welcome good Marcellus.

Mar. What, ha's this thing appear'd againe to night.

Bar. I haue seene nothing.

Mar. Horatio saies, 'tis but our Fantasie, And will not let beleefe take hold of him Touching this dreaded sight, twice seene of vs, Therefore I haue intreated him along With vs, to watch the minutes of this Night, That if againe this Apparition come, He may approue our eyes, and speake to it.

Hor. Tush, tush, 'twill not appeare.

Bar. Sit downe a-while, And let vs once againe assaile your eares, That are so fortified against our Story, What we two Nights haue seene.

Hor. Well, sit we downe, And let vs heare Barnardo speake of this.

Barn. Last night of all, When yond same Starre that's Westward from the Pole Had made his course t'illume that part of Heauen

Where now it burnes, Marcellus and my selfe, The Bell then beating one.

Mar. Peace, breake thee of: *Enter the Ghost.*
Looke where it comes againe.

Barn. In the same figure, like the King that's dead.

Mar. Thou art a Scholler; speake to it Horatio.

Barn. Lookes it not like the King? Marke it Horatio.

Hora. Most like: It harrowes me with fear & wonder

Barn. It would be spoke too.

Mar. Question it Horatio.

Hor. What art thou that vsurp'st this time of night, Together with that Faire and Warlike forme In which the Maiesty of buried Denmarke Did sometimes march: By Heauen I charge thee speake.

Mar. It is offended.

Barn. See, it stalkes away.

Hor. Stay: speake; speake: I Charge thee, speake.

Exit the Ghost.

Mar. 'Tis gone, and will not answer.

Barn. How now Horatio? You tremble & look pale: Is not this something more then Fantasie? What thinke you on't?

Hor. Before my God, I might not this beleeue Without the sensible and true auouch Of mine owne eyes.

Mar. Is it not like the King?

Hor. As thou art to thy selfe, Such was the very Armour he had on, When th'Ambitious Norwey combatted: So frown'd he once, when in an angry parle He smot the sledded Pollax on the Ice. 'Tis strange.

Mar. Thus twice before, and iust at this dead houre, With Martiall stalke, hath he gone by our Watch.

Hor. In what particular thought to work, I know not: But in the grosse and scope of my Opinion, This boades some strange erruption to our State.

Mar. Good now sit downe, & tell me he that knowes Why this same strict and most obseruant Watch, So nightly toyles the subiect of the Land, And why such dayly Cast of Brazon Cannon And Forraigne Mart for Implements of warre: Why such impresse of Ship-wrights, whose sore Taske Do's not diuide the Sunday from the weeke, What might be toward, that this sweaty hast Doth make the Night ioynt-Labourer with the day: Who is't that can informe me?

Hor. That can I,

At.

The Tragedy of Richard the Third:
with the Landing of Earle Richmond, and the Battell at Bosworth Field.

Actus Primus. Scœna Prima.

Enter Richard Duke of Gloster solus.

Ow is the Winter of our Discontent,
Made glorious Summer by this Son of Yorke:
And all the clouds that lowr'd vpon our house
In the deepe bosome of the Ocean buried.
Now are our browes bound with Victorious Wreathes,
Our bruised armes hung vp for Monuments;
Our sterne Alarums chang'd to merry Meetings;
Our dreadfull Marches, to delightfull Measures.
Grim-visag'd Warre, hath smooth'd his wrinkled Front:
And now, in stead of mounting Barbed Steeds,
To fright the Soules of fearfull Aduersaries,
He capers nimbly in a Ladies Chamber,
To the lasciuious pleasing of a Lute.
But I, that am not shap'd for sportiue trickes,
Nor made to court an amorous Looking-glasse:
I, that am Rudely stampt, and want loues Maiesty,
To strut before a wonton ambling Nymph:
I, that am curtail'd of this faire Proportion,
Cheated of Feature by dissembling Nature,
Deform'd, vn-finish'd, sent before my time
Into this breathing World, scarse halfe made vp,
And that so lamely and vnfashionable,
That dogges barke at me, as I halt by them.
Why I (in this weake piping time of Peace)
Haue no delight to passe away the time,
Vnlesse to see my Shadow in the Sunne,
And descant on mine owne Deformity.
And therefore, since I cannot proue a Louer,
To entertaine these faire well spoken dayes,
I am determined to proue a Villaine,
And hate the idle pleasures of these dayes.
Plots haue I laide, Inductions dangerous,
By drunken Prophesies, Libels, and Dreames,
To set my Brother Clarence and the King
In deadly hate, the one against the other:
And if King Edward be as true and iust,
As I am Subtle, False, and Treacherous,
This day should Clarence closely be mew'd vp:
About a Prophesie, which sayes that G,
Of Edwards heyres the murtherer shall be.
Diue thoughts downe to my soule, here Clarence comes.

Enter Clarence, and Brakenbury, guarded.
Brother, good day: What meanes this armed guard

That waites vpon your Grace?
Cla. His Maiesty tendring my persons safety,
Hath appointed this Conduct, to conuey me to th'Tower
Rich. Vpon what cause?
Cla. Because my name is George.
Rich. Alacke my Lord, that fault is none of yours:
He should for that commit your Godfathers.
O belike, his Maiesty hath some intent,
That you should be new Christned in the Tower.
But what's the matter Clarence, may I know?
Cla. Yea Richard, when I know: but I protest
As yet I do not; But as I can learne,
He hearkens after Prophesies and Dreames,
And from the Crosse-row pluckes the letter G:
And sayes, a Wizard told him, that by G,
His issue disinherited should be,
And for my name of George begins with G,
It followes in his thought, that I am he.
These (as I learne) and such like toyes as these,
Hath moou'd his Highnesse to commit me now.
Rich. Why this it is, when men are rul'd by Women:
'Tis not the King that sends you to the Tower,
My Lady Grey his Wife, Clarence tis shee,
That tempts him to this harsh Extremity.
Was it not shee, and that good man of Worship,
Anthony Woodeuile her Brother there,
That made him send Lord Hastings to the Tower?
From whence this present day he is deliuered?
We are not safe Clarence, we are not safe.
Cla. By heauen, I thinke there is no man secure
But the Queenes Kindred, and night-walking Heralds,
That trudge betwixt the King, and Mistris Shore.
Heard you not what an humble Suppliant
Lord Hastings was, for her deliuery?
Rich. Humbly complaining to her Deitie,
Got my Lord Chamberlaine his libertie,
Ile tell you what, I thinke it is our way,
If we will keepe in fauour with the King,
To be her men, and weare her Liuery.
The iealous ore-worne Widdow, and her selfe,
Since that our Brother dub'd them Gentlewomen,
Are mighty Gossips in our Monarchy.
Bra. I beseech your Graces both to pardon me,
His Maiesty hath straightly giuen in charge,
That no man shall haue priuate Conference
(Of what degree soeuer) with your Brother.

Rich.

The Famous History of the Life of
King HENRY the Eight.

THE PROLOGUE.

Come no more to make you Laugh, Things now,
That beare a Weighty, and a Serious Brow,
Sad, high, and working, full of State and Woe:
Such Noble Scænes, as draw the Eye to flow
We now present. Those that can Pitty, heere
May (if they thinke it well) let fall a Teare,
The Subiect will deserue it. Such as giue
Their Money out of hope they may beleeue,
May heere finde Truth too. Those that come to see
Onely a show or two, and so agree,
The Play may passe : If they be still, and willing,
Ile vndertake may see away their shilling
Richly in two short houres. Onely they
That come to heare a Merry, Bawdy Play,
A noyse of Targets : Or to see a Fellow
In a long Motley Coate, garded with Yellow,

Will be deceyu'd. For gentle Hearers, know
To ranke our chosen Truth with such a show
As Foole, and Fight is, beside forfeiting
Our owne Braines, and the Opinion that we bring
To make that onely true, we now intend,
Will leaue vs neuer an vnderstanding Friend.
Therefore, for Goodnesse sake, and as you are knowne
The First and Happiest Hearers of the Towne,
Be sad, as we would make ye. Thinke ye see
The very Persons of our Noble Story,
As they were Liuing : Thinke you see them Great,
And follow'd with the generall throng, and sweat
Of thousand Friends : Then, in a moment, see
How soone this Mightinesse, meets Misery :
And if you can be n euery then, Ile say,
A Man may weepe vpon his Wedding day.

Actus Primus. Scœna Prima.

Enter the Duke of Norfolke at one doore. At the other,
the Duke of Buckingham, and the Lord
Aburgauenny.

Buckingham.

Good morrow, and well met. How haue ye done
Since last we saw in France ?
Norf. I thanke your Grace :
Healthfull, and euer since a fresh Admirer
Of what I saw there.
Buck. An vntimely Ague
Staid me a Prisoner in my Chamber, when
Those Sunnes of Glory, those two Lights of Men
Met in the vale of Andren.
Nor. 'Twixt Guynes and Arde,
I was then present, saw them salute on Horsebacke,
Beheld them when they lighted, how they clung
In their Embracement, as they grew together,
Which had they,
What foure Thron'd ones could haue weigh'd
Such a compounded one ?
Buck. All the whole time
I was my Chambers Prisoner.

Nor. Then you lost
The view of earthly glory : Men might say
Till this time Pompe was single, but now married
To one aboue it selfe. Each following day
Became the next dayes master, till the last
Made former Wonders, it's. To day the French,
All Clinquant all in Gold, like Heathen Gods
Shone downe the English ; and to morrow, they
Made Britaine, India : Euery man that stood,
Shew'd like a Mine. Their Dwarfish Pages were
As Cherubins, all gilt : the Madams too,
Not vs'd to toyle, did almost sweat to beare
The Pride vpon them, that their very labour
Was to them, as a Painting. Now this Maske
Was cry'de Incompareable ; and th'ensuing night
Made it a Foole, and Begger. The two Kings
Equall in lustre, were now best, now worst
As presence did present them : Him in eye,
Still him in praise, and being present both,
'Twas said they saw but one, and no Discerner
Durst wagge his Tongue in censure, when these Sunnes
(For so they phrase 'em) by their Heralds challeng'd
The Noble Spirits to Armes, they did performe

Beyond

THE TRAGEDIE OF
KING LEAR.

Actus Primus. Scœna Prima.

Enter Kent, Gloucester, and Edmond.

Kent.

I Thought the King had more affected the
Duke of *Albany*, then *Cornwall*.

Glou. It did alwayes seeme so to vs : But
now in the diuision of the Kingdome, it appeares not which of the Dukes hee valewes
most, for qualities are so weigh'd, that curiosity in nei-
ther, can make choise of eithers moity.

Kent. Is not this your Son, my Lord ?

Glou. His breeding Sir, hath bin at my charge. I haue
so often blush'd to acknowledge him, that now I am
braz'd too't.

Kent. I cannot conceiue you.

Glou. Sir, this yong Fellowes mother could ; where-
vpon she grew round womb'd, and had indeede (Sir) a
Sonne for her Cradle, ere she had a husband for her bed.
Do you smell a fault ?

Kent. I cannot wish the fault vndone, the issue of it,
being so proper.

Glou. But I haue a Sonne, Sir, by order of Law, some
yeere elder then this ; who, yet is no deerer in my ac-
count, though this Knaue came somthing sawcily to the
world before he was sent for : yet was his Mother fayre,
there was good sport at his making, and the horson must
be acknowledged. Doe you know this Noble Gentleman, *Edmond* ?

Edm. No, my Lord.

Glou. My Lord of Kent :
Remember him heereafter, as my Honourable Friend.

Edm. My seruices to your Lordship.

Kent. I must loue you, and sue to know you better.

Edm. Sir, I shall study deseruing.

Glou. He hath bin out nine yeares, and away he shall
againe. The King is comming.

Sennet. Enter King Lear, Cornwall, Albany, Gonerill, Re-
gan, Cordelia, and attendants.

Lear. Attend the Lords of France & Burgundy, Glofter.

Glou. I shall, my Lord.   *Exit.*

Lear. Meane time we shal expresse our darker purpose.
Giue me the Map there. Know, that we haue diuided
In three our Kingdome : and 'tis our fast intent,
To shake all Cares and Businesse from our Age,
Conferring them on yonger strengths, while we
Vnburthen'd crawle toward death. Our son of *Cornwal*,
And you our no lesse louing Sonne of *Albany*,

We haue this houre a constant will to publish
Our daughters seuerall Dowers, that future strife
May be preuented now. The Princes, *France* & *Burgundy*,
Great Riuals in our yongest daughters loue,
Long in our Court, haue made their amorous soiourne,
And heere are to be answer'd. Tell me my daughters
(Since now we will diuest vs both of Rule,
Interest of Territory, Cares of State)
Which of you shall we say doth loue vs most,
That we, our largest bountie may extend
Where Nature doth with merit challenge. *Gonerill*,
Our eldest borne, speake first.

Gon. Sir, I loue you more then word can weild ƒ matter,
Deerer then eye-sight, space, and libertie,
Beyond what can be valewed, rich or rare,
No lesse then life, with grace, health, beauty, honor :
As much as Childe ere lou'd, or Father found.
A loue that makes breath poore, and speech vnable,
Beyond all manner of so much I loue you.

Cor. What shall *Cordelia* speake ? Loue, and be silent.

Lear. Of all these bounds euen from this Line, to this,
With shadowie Forrests, and with Champains rich'd
With plenteous Riuers, and wide-skirted Meades
We make thee Lady. To thine and *Albanies* issues
Be this perpetuall. What sayes our second Daughter?
Our deerest *Regan*, wife of *Cornwall* ?

Reg. I am made of that selfe-mettle as my Sister,
And prize me at her worth. In my true heart,
I finde she names my very deede of loue :
Onely she comes too short, that I professe
My selfe an enemy to all other ioyes,
Which the most precious square of sense professes,
And finde I am alone felicitate
In your deere Highnesse loue.

Cor. Then poore *Cordelia*,
And yet not so, since I am sure my loue's
More ponderous then my tongue.

Lear. To thee, and thine hereditarie euer,
Remaine this ample third of our faire Kingdome,
No lesse in space, validitie, and pleasure
Then that conferr'd on *Gonerill*. Now our Ioy,
Although our last and least ; to whose yong loue,
The Vines of France, and Milke of Burgundie,
Striue to be interest. What can you say, to draw
A third, more opilent then your Sisters? speake.

Cor. Nothing my Lord.

Lear. Nothing ?

THE TRAGEDIE OF
Othello, the Moore of Venice.

Actus Primus. Scœna Prima.

Enter Rodorigo, and Iago.

Roderigo.

NEuer tell me, I take it much vnkindly
That thou (*Iago*) who haft had my purſe,
As if ſ ſtrings were thine, ſhould'ſt know of this.

Ia. But you'l not beare me. If euer I did dream
Of ſuch a matter, abhorre me.

Rodo. Thou told'ſt me,
Thou did'ſt hold him in thy hate.

Iago. Deſpiſe me
If I do not. Three Great-ones of the Cittie,
(In perſonall ſuite to make me his Lieutenant)
Off-capt to him: and by the faith of man
I know my price, I am worth no worſſe a place.
But he (as louing his owne pride, and purpoſes)
Euades them, with a bumbaſt Circumſtance,
Horribly ſtufft with Epithites of warre,
Non-ſuites my Mediators. For certes, ſaies he,
I haue already choſe my Officer. And what was he?
For-ſooth, a great Arithmatician,
One *Michaell Caſſio*, a *Florentine*,
(A Fellow almoſt damn'd in a faire Wife)
That neuer ſet a Squadron in the Field,
Nor the deuiſion of a Battaile knowes
More then a Spinſter. Vnleſſe the Bookiſh Theoricke:
Wherein the Tongued Conſuls can propoſe
As Maſterly as he. Meere pratle (without practiſe)
Is all his Souldierſhip. But he (Sir) had th'election;
And I (of whom his eies had ſeene the proofe
At Rhodes, at Ciprus, and on others grounds
Chriſten'd, and Heathen muſt be be-leed, and calm'd
By Debitor, and Creditor. This Counter-caſter,
He (in good time) muſt his Lieutenant be,
And I (bleſſe the marke) his Moorſhips Auntient.

Rod. By heauen, I rather would haue bin his hangman.

Iago. Why, there's no remedie.
'Tis the curſſe of Seruice;
Preferment goes by Letter, and affection,
And not by old gradation, where each ſecond
Stood Heire to th'firſt. Now Sir, be iudge your ſelfe,
Whether I in any iuſt terme am Affin'd
To loue the *Moore*?

Rod. I would not follow him then.

Iago. O Sir content you.
I follow him, to ſerue my turne vpon him.
We cannot all be Maſters, nor all Maſters
Cannot be truely follow'd. You ſhall marke
Many a durious and knee-crooking knaue;
That (doting on his owne obſequious bondage)
Weares out his time, much like his Maſters Aſſe,
For naught but Prouender, & when he's old Caſheer'd.
Whip me ſuch honeſt knaues. Others there are
Who trym'd in Formes, and viſages of Dutie,
Keepe yet their hearts attending on themſelues,
And throwing but ſhowes of Seruice on their Lords
Doe well thriue by them.
And when they haue lin'd their Coates
Doe themſelues Homage.
Theſe Fellowes haue ſome ſoule,
And ſuch a one do I profeſſe my ſelfe. For (Sir)
It is as ſure as you are *Rodorigo*,
Were I the Moore, I would not be *Iago*:
In following him, I follow but my ſelfe.
Heauen is my Iudge, not I for loue and dutie,
But ſeeming ſo, for my peculiar end:
For when my outward Action doth demonſtrate
The natiue act, and figure of my heart
In Complement externe, 'tis not long after
But I will weare my heart vpon my ſleeue
For Dawes to pecke at; I am not what I am.

Rod. What a full Fortune do's the Thicks-lips owe
If he can carry't thus?

Iago. Call vp her Father:
Rowſe him, make after him, poyſon his delight,
Proclaime him in the Streets. Incenſe her kinſmen,
And though he in a fertile Clymate dwell,
Plague him with Flies: though that his Ioy be Ioy,
Yet throw ſuch chances of vexation on't,
As it may looſe ſome colour.

Rodo. Heere is her Fathers houſe, I'le call aloud.

Iago. Doe, with like timerous accent, and dire yell,
As when (by Night and Negligence) the Fire
Is ſpied in populus Citties.

Rodo. What hoa: Brabantio, Signior *Brabantio*, hoa.

Iago. Awake: what hoa, *Brabantio*: Theeues, Theeues.
Looke to your houſe, your daughter, and your Bags,
Theeues, Theeues.

Bra. Aboue. What is the reaſon of this terrible
Summons? What is the matter there?

Rodo. Signior is all your Familie within?

Iago. Are your Doores lock'd?

Bra. Why? Wherefore aſk you this?

Iago. Sir, y'are rob'd, for ſhame put on your Gowne,
Your

The Workes of William Shakespeare,

containing all his Comedies, Histories, and
Tragedies: Truely set forth, according to their first
ORIGINALL.

The Names of the Principall Actors
in all these Playes.

William Shakespeare.

Richard Burbadge.

John Hemmings.

Augustine Phillips.

William Kempt.

Thomas Poope.

George Bryan.

Henry Condell.

William Slye.

Richard Cowly.

John Lowine.

Samuell Crosse.

Alexander Cooke.

Samuel Gilburne.

Robert Armin.

William Ostler.

Nathan Field.

John Underwood.

Nicholas Tooley.

William Ecclestone.

Joseph Taylor.

Robert Benfield.

Robert Goughe.

Richard Robinson.

Iohn Shancke.

Iohn Rice.